SUPER SPUNKY
Grandmas
And Other Amusing Stuff

KEN MOGREN

For information, contact
MSI Press, LLC
1760-F Airline Hwy #203
Hollister, CA 95023

Copyeditor: Betty Lou Leaver
Cover Design & Layout: Opeyemi Ikuborije
Front Cover Image: Joella Goyette
Chapter Illustrations: Joelle Goyette

LCCN: 2024911960
ISBN: 978-1-957354-46-0

To Spunky Grandmas Everywhere

CONTENTS

Preface

After my previous book, *Spunky Grandmas...And Other Amusing Characters*, was released, I had many opportunities to share my creations with live audiences. I quickly learned it was important to assure the audience right away that they were not trapped in a poetry reading. Most people aren't real fond of poetry, so let me assure you that what follows is not like what comes to mind when you hear the P word.

I write sonnets in a genre called "humorous verse." That means there's rhythm and rhyme, like Dr. Seuss and Mother Goose and unlike a lot of the free verse poetry written today. I tell stories and deliver messages in clear, simple language. Any beautiful imagery or clever metaphors are strictly coincidental. Back when I took poetry classes in school, I was pretty oblivious to symbolism and hidden meanings and was baffled by references to Greek mythology and many other things I was ignorant of. So, I keep it simple and try to make it humorous or at least amusing.

I'm an admirer of Mark Twain who is acknowledged by many as America's greatest humorist. Like Twain, I believe that truly good humor has to include some element of truth. I think you'll find a lot of truth about human nature and our culture in the sonnets that follow.

Why sonnets? I enjoy the challenge of fitting a story or message into just 14 lines while obeying all of the "rules" about rhyme and meter. I hope you enjoy reading them as much as I enjoy writing them.

Chapter 1
SUPER SPUNKY
Grandmas

Super Spunky Grandmas
Chapter Notes

The grandmas in the stories that follow aren't much like a stereotype that still exists to some extent. Grandmas today have been liberated from the expectations that shaped the lives of their own grandmas. Some are more liberated and less inhibited than others. These are their stories. Remember, most stories are improved with a bit of exaggeration.

TRAFFIC STOP

While doing forty in a thirty zone,
Her rearview mirror lit up red and blue.
The cop had also seen her on her phone,
But Grandma knew some things that she could do.

The cop strode up and said, "Your license, please."
She said, "I think I knew you as a kid."
The cop said, "Got no time to shoot the breeze.
I gotta ticket you for what you did."

But Granny knew a way when things look grim,
To change the mind of any traffic cop.
She reached into her purse and handed him
A gift card for a local doughnut shop.

"Just be more careful," he was heard to say
Before he took the card and drove away,

SUPER SPUNKY GRANDMAS BOOK CLUB

Six super spunky grandmas like to meet
To talk about some books they all had read.
There's always wine and tasty things to eat,
And sometimes gossip fills the room instead.

The books they choose are anything but tame.
They have no time for girly, feel good fluff.
They like romance with cheating, lust, and shame
And mostly talk about the trashy stuff.

As wine goes down, it lightens up the mood.
The laughs get loud and speech becomes more slurred.
Well-mannered discourse oft becomes more crude
As comments on the book grow more absurd.

There have been times the meeting went 'til dawn.
They never end 'til all the wine is gone.

EX-SMOKER

She hasn't smoked since nineteen ninety-eight.
Now grandma thinks that everyone should quit.
There's no tobacco smoke she doesn't hate.
She's nauseated by the smell of it.

Her balcony is on the second floor.
A guy who just moved in and smokes a lot
Lives just below and smokes outside his door.
He now regrets he got her temper hot.

The next time that he stepped outside to smoke,
She dumped a pail of water on his head.
Surprised, he asked, "Is this some sort of joke?"
She said, "Stop smoking, or you'll end up dead.

"My health and yours are what I care about.
Each time you smoke, that's how I'll put it out."

ANNOYING FELLOW PASSENGER

She sat beside a stranger on a plane
Who soon had Grandma feeling quite annoyed.
His uninvited comments were a pain
Cuz politics she chooses to avoid.

His views were vastly different from her own,
Hers in the middle, his beyond extreme.
Her anger grew as on and on he'd drone,
But when he slept, she carried out a scheme.

She found a flight attendant and complained,
"A terrorist is seated in my row.
He's made alarming comments," she explained.
"Officials where we're landing need to know."

And when they reached the ground, it made her day
To see him placed in cuffs and led away.

GARBAGE-MOUTH GRANNY

The F word was the word she used the most.
Habitually, she'd always find a way
In spoken word or written Facebook post
To utilize it scores of times each day.

She liked it as an adjective and verb.
She used out as an expletive, of course.
And as a noun, she thought it was superb,
But one day she began to feel remorse.

She'd heard an F-bomb from her grandson's lips,
And for the first time, felt a bit of shame.
His folks would deem it an apocalypse.
So, she was ready when she got the blame.

She told them, "You can blame that damned TV.
It sure as hell could not have come from me."

GRANDMA'S SHOULDER PAIN

She told the doc, "My shoulder hurts like hell.
This left one, damned thing wakes me up at night.
You gotta find a way to get it well."
The doc said, "I will try to make it right."

He twisted, poked, and bent the joint around,
Then said, "I think you're screwed. It's just old age,
For which a remedy has ne'er been found."
This launched the gal into a fit of rage.

She told the doc, "I think that you're a quack."
"How dare you you question me!" the doctor said.
Unshaken, she continued her attack.
"I doubt you've got a brain inside your head!

"You're wrong about the theory you assert.
The right one's just as old but doesn't hurt."

OPTIMISTIC GRANDMA

A grandma woke, prepared to seize the day,
Believing only good things lay ahead.
But had she known what woes would come her way,
It would have paid to simply stay in bed.

By noon she'd stepped in dog poop, lost her keys,
Had dropped her cell phone, shattering the screen,
Was stung while walking through a swarm of bees,
And got the trots from Mexican cuisine.

And though things worsened as the day progressed,
She didn't bellyache or curse her fate.
While normal people would have felt depressed,
She shrugged it off and said, "I'm feelin' great!

"Cuz bad things happen. Things could be much worse.
I could be horizontal in a hearse."

GRANDMA'S NEW CAR DILEMMA

She's hesitant to buy a brand-new car
Cuz tech proficiency is now a must.
For her, technology has gone too far
And left her sadly standing in the dust.

She'd rather turn a dial than touch a screen.
She much prefers a button, switch, or knob.
On most things digital, she's not too keen.
She'd rather use a key than trust a fob.

Should she just keep her relic from the past?
New cars do lots of stuff she doesn't need.
They make her feel dimwitted and harassed.
Her message auto makers ought to heed:

"You idiots! Why is it you can't see
You need to dumb it down for folks like me!"

AGE OR WEIGHT

A carnival had just arrived in town.
A little boy asked, "Grandma, can we go?"
She didn't want to let her grandson down.
When grandkids ask, a grandma can't say no.

He said to Grandma, "Wouldn't it be great
If you could win for me a teddy bear?"
She saw a game called Guess Your Age or Weight.
She hatched a plan and wandered over there.

"Guess thirty-nine, and I'll take care of you?
She whispered to the carney with a wink.
She slipped him fifty. He knew what to do.
"Wrong guess!" she said. "I'm older than you think,"

And as the bear was handed to the boy,
The carney winked. Her bribe had brought joy.

Chapter 2
Geezers

Geezers Chapter Notes

There doesn't seem to be universal agreement on whether the term "geezer" is derogatory or not. In this chapter, it is not. I think of a geezer as an older gentleman whose get-up-and-go has got up and gone, but perhaps he doesn't know it yet. He might dodder a bit, be a little absent minded, and grumble from time to time, but he's far from a cranky curmudgeon. I find geezers to be amusing characters and hope you are amused by the stories that follow.

GEEZER COFFEE KLATSCH

Retired and bored with lots of time to waste,
A coffee klatsch of geezers meets each day.
They drink cheap coffee, gripe about the taste,
And shoot the breeze to fritter time away.

From day to day, the topics stay the same:
Their aches and pains, the weather if it's bad,
The local team that lost and who's to blame,
And stuff that's in the news that makes them mad.

A guy who always has a joke to tell
Gets full attention when he has the floor.
Alas, he can't remember very well
And might tell one he told the week before.

But others laugh as though it's all brand new,
For they have all become forgetful too.

POKER WITH GHOSTS

In Ernie's basement they had played for years,
Six guys who liked their weekly poker game.
They talked some trash and polished off some beers,
But winning cash from others was their aim.

Old age caught up with one who liked to play,
And though his death made others feel bereft,
The games went on 'til five had passed away,
And Ernie was the only player left.

He'd deal six hands, with five to empty chairs
And put a pile of money at each spot.
He'd play his hand but also manage theirs
In such a way that he won every pot.

He thought this new approach was much more fun.
When they were all alive, he rarely won.

RECOLLECTION ENIGMA

A geezer seems to easily recall
Events that happened many years ago.
But when he's finished shopping at the mall,
To find his car, he wanders to and fro.

The places and the faces from his past
Are vivid images within his brain.
While way-back recollections seem to last,
Recalling recent stuff can be a pain.

He can't remember where he put his keys
Or conversations held just yesterday,
Which often leaves him feeling ill at ease.
So, why do human brains behave this way?

Perhaps they're like a filing cabinet drawer,
When they get full, they have no room for more.

YOU CAN'T TAKE IT WITH YOU

A saying long regarded to be true
Is, "You can't take it with you when you die."
A grumpy geezer who was well-to-do
Decided it was something he would try.

He hatched a clever plan as he grew old.
He had no friends or children in his life.
He'd transfer all his assets into gold
Except a single dime for his ex-wife.

He hired a metal sculptor. Then, he said,
"Take all this gold and make an ashes urn.
Then, drop it in the ocean when I'm dead
So deep there ain't no way 'twill e'er return.

The sculptor stole the gold which proves it's true:
It's hard to take your wealth along with you.

WIFE WANTED

A geezer who had always loved to fish
Had been, by choice, unmarried all his life.
Arthritis and bad eyesight made him wish
That he could find a caring, helpful wife.

A newspaper he bought and read each day
Contained a column called "Ask Juliet,"
Advice on romance that might light his way.
He'd welcome any insight he could get.

He wrote, "Wife wanted. Don't care how she looks,
But she will need to learn to drive a boat,
Back trailers up and bait my fishing hooks."
It made her column. Here is what she wrote:

"Hey, fish guy, you won't find those kind of brides,
But try the want ads under Fishing Guides.

FRUMPY GEEZER'S NEW CORVETTE

When young, he never had a flashy car
But always dreamed he'd own a red Corvette.
If what you drive tells people who you are,
He knew the Vette was what he had to get.

He'd worked hard all his life and had success.
'Twas time to show the world his dashing style.
He didn't know 'twould turn out such a mess
But found out ere he'd gone a single mile.

He stopped beside two hotties at a light.
They saw the car and gawked to check him out.
Their look of disappointment at his sight
Caused all his confidence to turn to doubt.

He ought regret the car he chose to buy.
In truth, he'd just a Prius sort of guy.

THE SOURCE OF WISDOM

An older gent, reputed to be wise,
Was asked how all his wisdom was acquired.
He answered, "This may come as a surprise,
But giant intellect is not required.

"It can't be gained from books and can't be taught.
It's not determined by your DNA.
And wealth won't do it. Wisdom can't be bought.
To get it, there's a different price to pay.

"My wisdom came from doing stupid stuff,
Like quitting school and getting thrown in jail.
When drinking, I could never get enough.
I lost some jobs and had my marriage fail.

"If you seek wisdom, all it really takes
Is learning from a bunch of dumb mistakes."

Chapter 3
The Written Word

.

The Written Word
Chapter Notes

I was inspired to write sonnets because my home town, Winona, Minnesota, is home to the Great River Shakespeare Festival. Because Shakespeare wrote a lot of sonnets, the festival, in addition to staging plays, holds a sonnet writing contest each year. The first two sonnets in this chapter were the first two I ever wrote, and both were contest entries. Winona also has a Beethoven festival which the first sonnet alludes to. The second speculates facetiously that Shakespeare was the father of rap music. I don't believe Shakespeare ever wrote a sonnet about loose women, so the third imagines what such a sonnet might have looked like. The rest of the chapter deals with other forms of written words.

SUMMER ENTERTAINMENT IN WINONA

In days gone by, we watched our baseball Chiefs.
It was a pleasant summer thing to do.
But now it seems we've altered our beliefs,
For there are newly added choices, too.

The Bard hit town, and much like Harold Hill,
He cast a spell upon the local folks.
It seems we've all become new fans of Will,
Though some of us don't always get his jokes.

And then this guy named Ludwig came along.
He's famous, and his symphonies are great.
Which form of art is right and which is wrong?
I say both delight and captivate.

No need for conflict, arguments, and fights.
Let's watch them both on alternating nights.

SHAKESPEARIAN RAP

Just found amongst some sixteenth century crap,
This Shakespeare poem reveals the roots of Rap:

"I'm Will. I write the plays and, dude, I'm good!
So say the knaves and varlets from the hood.
Cheap laughs, a bit of raunch, a little gore
Are all it takes to make my homies roar.
Some dukes and lords show up but aren't as loud.
They're doubtlessly outnumbered in the crowd."

But somewhere through the years the fan base changed.
The lowlife, highbrow mix was rearranged.
The audience of ordinary slobs
Was crowded out by snooty, cultured snobs.
Except Winona somehow got it right.
You'll find all types on any given night.

ELIZABETHAN PUB FLOOZIE

Shall I compare thee to a pint of ale?
Thy charms are tempting, like a bag of chips.
Alas, consumption of these never fail
To add some extra padding to thy hips.

Thy beauty fades by day but shines at night.
It shineth most when closing time drawth near,
When drunken, lustful knaves assume the right
To whisper lies they think thou yearnst to hear.

These varlets' words can turn a maiden's head.
Thou know'st, of course, their talk of love's not true,
Just trickery to get thee into bed.
Still, they get what they want. But thou dost, too!

If ale be what thee ought be likened to,
Thou art like rancid, skunky tasting brew.

A SONNET ABOUT LIMERICKS

A type of poem most anyone can write,
The limerick. It's only five lines long.
But if you want to write one, do it right.
Just heed this simple rule. You can't go wrong.

A limerick should be a bit obscene.
That's what most any reader will expect.
Your poem won't seem as funny if it's clean,
And that's a simple truth you must accept.

Most any raunchy subject ought to do.
There's lots of things we label as bad taste.
The one you choose is strictly up to you,
But decency is just poetic waste.

To read or hear a limerick that's clean,
Is much like coffee made without caffein.

TOO MANY CLICHES?

The overuse of buzz words and cliches
Should always be avoided like the plague.
We all are bored to tears by such a phrase,
And many old as dirt cliches are vague.

Suppose you have an awesome thought to share.
You want to be profound and crystal clear.
You've wracked your brain for words with zing and flair
But drawn a blank. You've had it up to here!

When at wit's end, the wind gone from your sails,
Just knuckle down and think outside the box,
A tried and true approach that never fails.
For sure, you'll coin a phrase that really rocks.

The group of words that you combine today
Might just become tomorrow's new cliche.

CLASSIC COUNTRY MUSIC

You want to write a classic country song?
You first must choose a subject from this list:
Like cheatin' men who've done their women wrong,
Or vengeance when mistreated gals get pissed.

You might explain mens' love of pickup trucks
Or pine about a trailer repossessed.
Folks love a song about a job that sucks
Or beer on Friday nights when life is best.

A formula that's worked well through the years
Is using worn-out rhymes to show your wit.
Take "drink'n'/think'n," throw in "beers and tears,"
Add "bar stool/damn fool." You might have a hit.

Remember not to revel but to moan,
Half-empty, not half-full, should be the tone.

Chapter 4
FOOD AND DRINK

Food and Drink
Chapter Notes

It seems that enjoying food and drink is one of America's greatest pastimes. That's what the stories in this chapter are about. If there is a common theme running through them, it's that we have a tendency to indulge in food and drink to excess.

BETCHA CAN'T BURGER

You win a T-shirt if you finish one,
Though two XL's the smallest size they stock.
The Betcha Can't's a feat that's rarely done
'Cuz it requires you also beat the clock.

You get just half an hour to eat it all.
It's big around as any dinner plate.
Four twelve-ounce patties, seven inches tall.
For most who try, the task is far too great.

Before you start, you sign a full release.
It's almost certain something bad awaits.
The more you eat the more, the odds increase.
It either makes you barf or constipates.

It seems some people just aren't smart enough
To keep from trying really stupid stuff.

FOOD PORTIONS

The thing that I dislike when dining out
Is when the portion sizes are so big.
It's like they want for me to have the gout
Or think they need to feed me like a pig.

Small wonder more of us are now obese,
Within those giant servings, bad things lurk.
There's sugar, fat, and salt fried up in grease.
It makes our gastric systems overwork.

There is, of course, the opposite extreme—,
Those pricey gourmet joints that ration food.
While snooty foodies praise this stingy scheme,
I go home hungry in an angry mood.

So, I'll go where I need a doggy bag.
Big portions get my pooch's tail to wag.

TWELVE PACK OF BEER

The first beer's always great for quenching thirst.
It often tells the brain, "Let's have some more."
The second's even better than the first,
Which sometimes leads to having three or four.

With number five, there comes a pleasant buzz,
And number six makes troubles disappear.
The seventh can be dangerous because
It's when a person's thinking gets less clear.

Perceived intelligence arrives with eight.
Our looks improve a lot if we've had nine.
With ten we're bulletproof and feeling great
But past the point we should have drawn the line.

Don't drink the final two 'cuz they're a curse.
They'll make tomorrow's headache even worse.

BUFFET BUFFOON

A glutton on a ten-day ocean cruise
Became a fixture at the ship's buffet.
Ignoring other options he could choose,
He'd fill his plate a dozen times a day.

He elbowed, pushed, and shoved to cut the line.
His fellow passengers grew much annoyed.
He'd sneer as if to say, "This food's all mine,"
And soon became a nuisance to avoid.

The captain and the crew were much alarmed.
His bad behavior couldn't be ignored.
Their training stressed that guests should not be harmed,
Or they'd have gladly thrown him overboard.

So, he kept eating, adding to his girth.
Some folks just have to get their money's worth.

IN PRAISE OF COFFEE

A special gift from God, the coffee bean,
Bestowed around the world for all mankind.
The source of an elixir called caffeine,
It activates and stimulates the mind.

Like rocket fuel, it helps us launch the day,
It causes vim and vigor to abound,
And if we need a boost along the way,
Another cup gives power to astound.

But some folks shun the magic it affords.
Alas, they make a terrible mistake
To foolishly forego caffeine's rewards
For fear at bedtime they'll be wide awake.

If forced to drink their decaf stuff instead,
Like zombies, we'd become the walking dead.

WINE SNOBS

A guy who never really cared for wine
Had always been a bigger fan of beer.
His boss said, "Take some clients out to dine."
A bunch of wine snobs, it became quite clear.

Each twirled and swirled their glass held by its stem.
They talked about the legs and the bouquet.
It wasn't long 'til he grew bored with them.
Alas, they all still had a lot to say.

One took a sip and said, "It's coarse and dry."
Another said. "It's nutty, rough. and firm."
"A bit herbaceous," said another guy.
Perplexed, their baffled host began to squirm.

When he was asked for comments, he turned red.
"I think it tastes a lot like grapes." he said.

HEALTHY FOOD FANATIC

He didn't drink and always watched his weight.
Good health was something he obsessed about.
He woke up every morning feeling great.
He'd outlive friends. There wasn't any doubt.

Fastidious about the foods he chose,
Organic stuff was mostly what he'd eat.
Detesting trans fats, salt, and GMOs,
He ate a lot of fish and not much meat.

It seemed for sure he'd live a lengthy life.
But best laid plans, alas, don't always work,
And no one lives completely free from strife.
The world's a place where many dangers lurk.

Longevity in part depends on luck.
At fifty, he was flattened by a truck.

Chapter 5
OBSERVATIONS OF LIFE ON EARTH

Observations of Life on Earth
Chapter Notes

If someone from a distant planet was thinking about relocating to Earth and wanted to understand what life here is like, they would get some sense of our culture and the nature of human behavior from the stories in this chapter. It's hard to predict if we'd get any inter-planetary migrants. It would probably depend on how the quirkiness of the two planets compares.

SUPERMARKET TABLOIDS

Those lurid tabloids in the check-out lane
Have shocking headlines meant to turn your head,
Like "SCANDAL ROCKS POLITICAL CAMPAIGN,"
Or "COUSIN SWEARS THAT ELVIS ISN'T DEAD."

"EXPECT INVASION SOON FROM OUTER SPACE."
"DID CIA KILL MARILYN MONROE?"
"WHY ROCK STAR PUNCHED HIS GIRL FRIEND
IN THE FACE."
The stuff they think that people need to know.

They publish things that others wouldn't dare.
Detractors find them easy to malign,
But grocery shoppers hardly seem to care.
They entertain us while we stand in line.

Of course, it's bogus, but you might agree
It's not much worse than news that's on TV.

WALMART JOKES

It seems we never tire of Walmart jokes.
Its customers are cleverly maligned,
Depicted as a bunch of oddball folks
Or picked apart for being unrefined.

The folks we see in videos and memes
Have weird tattoos and butt cracks on display.
There's cleavage, clothing bursting at the seams,
And multicolored hair in disarray.

A lot of groups that claim to be maligned
Demand that people give them more respect,
But Walmart patrons hardly seem to mind,
And gripe about it less than you'd expect.

Since most of us have bought from Walmart's shelves,
Perhaps we're really laughing at ourselves.

DUMB DESTINATIONS

A travel agent looking to get rich
Promoted tours that fizzled every time.
But then one day he thought he'd found his niche.
He'd line up trips to spots with names that rhyme.

Nebraska to Alaska was his first.
Savannah to Havana was a hit.
Crimea/North Korea was the worst,
A bad mistake he'll readily admit.

Success resumed again with Maine to Spain.
Rwanda to Uganda was a dud
And Syria/Siberia insane,
Then Pakistan/Iran produced some blood.

If he would read the news he'd surely know
The places tourists really shouldn't go.

PANDEMIC PRECAUTIONS

A deadly viral threat arrived one day.
Twas killing thousands in the ICU.
A frantic search began to find a way
To keep us safe and thwart the bugaboo.

We hunkered down, used masks when we went out,
Wore gloves at first to push a shopping cart,
Avoided risks where safety was in doubt,
Then washed our hands, and stayed six feet apart.

But were precautions worse than the disease?
The crisis altered every part of life.
The deadly menace kept us ill at ease,
Yet, something good emerged from all the strife.

We learned how hard it is to live without
A lot of stuff we once complained about.

TOILET PAPER HOARDER

A man possessed by Covid-19 fears
Went out each day to every store in town,
Bought toilet paper he could use for years,
And when he had enough, he hunkered down.

But thoughts of diarrhea made him fret.
He felt a need to add to his supply,
And even though he had to go in debt,
His online search found more that he could buy.

The Fed Ex trucks unloaded every day,
The Charmin coming in a huge barrage.
It took him hours to put it all away.
He filled his storeroom, basement and garage.

So, he won't have to buy the stuff again
Unless he lives to be a hundred ten.

SNOW DAY

The forecast said there'd be a foot of snow.
There was no doubt. The clouds were thick and gray.
To make things worse, the wind was 'sposed to blow,
So, school officials said, " No school today."

Instead of staying in from winter's blast
The kids got out toboggans, skis and sleds,
And many either wound up in a cast
Or got concussions when they banged their heads.

The older kids sought other types of fun.
The ones with fake I.D.s were in the bars.
Some partied, and before the storm was done
Some girls got pregnant. Others crashed their cars.

While kids all think a snow day's really cool.
Despite the snow, they're far more safe in school.

PARENTAL LIES

Most parents tell their kids a bunch of lies
'Bout Santa and his reindeer, elves, and sleigh.
But when the truth comes out, it's no surprise
Some kids lose trust in what their parents say.

They lie about a lot of other things.
A stork had brought their siblings, so they said.
They talked of stuff the Easter Bunny brings,
And those are not the only lies they've spread.

Most kids aren't hard to fool when four years old,
But as they age, it doesn't take a sleuth
To stop believing lies that they've been told,
Like fairies paying when they lose a tooth.

And so perhaps it's really not so odd
Some kids grow up who don't believe in God.

POLITICAL INSULTS

Two candidates who sought to win a seat
Had views on issues that were much the same.
So, other ways were needed to compete,
And insults back and forth became the game.

She never failed to blast him when she spoke.
"He beats his wife. The guy's a total bum.
He's ugly, and his combover's a joke.
He's crooked, lazy, arrogant, and dumb."

So, in return he'd go on the attack.
"She's taken bribes. Her wealth she won't disclose.
Her plastic surgeon has to be a quack.
Her face looks like it melted, then refroze."

When votes were cast, and all was said and done,
Turns out a less known, write-in, person won.

ENDLESS SUMMER

Those guys who harmonized, " I Get Around "
Were handsome, young, and tan with smiles like pearls.
They had the fastest set of wheels in town
And turned the heads of California girls.

They'd rather catch a wave than be in school
Or feel some good vibrations in the sun,
And cruisin' in their four-oh-nine was cool.
All Summer long they lived for fun, fun, fun.

But now they're old and wrinkled, bald or gray.
Their longtime, loyal fans look much the same.
In time, the Beach Boys all must pass away,
But it's for sure they won't outlive their fame.

And still they play for aging Boomer throngs,
Made young again each time they hear those songs

Chapter 6
AS SEEN ON TV

As Seen On Tv
Chapter Notes

It seems there have traditionally been two categories of stuff shown on TV, commercials and other content. So, it's fitting that the stories in this chapter are either about commercials or other stuff. I'm a little old fashioned and have yet to embrace commercial-free streaming in a big way. I don't detest commercials because they provide potty breaks, and some are pretty entertaining. I hope you are entertained by the stories in this chapter.

TV DRUG ADS

She watched a lot of drug ads on TV
That claimed to cure a host of nasty ills.
She thought, "Those ailments sound a lot like me.
I've got to get prescriptions for those pills."

She saw her doc and brought along a list.
He said, "You don't need any of this stuff."
And though the lady started to insist,
He said, "You're healthy, and I've heard enough. "

He added that "The one thing wrong with you
Is you've been watching way too much TV.
Heed this advice about what you should do,
And you'll feel better. That's a guarantee.

"Each time one of those pesky ads appears,
You need to shut your eyes and plug your ears."

DOES ANYONE REMEMBER RON POPEIL

Does anyone remember Ron Popeil?
You might if more than thirty-five years old.
A master of the pitchman's smooth-talk spiel,
He turned some cheesy products into gold.

The Ronco Chop-O-Matic was the first.
His Pocket Fisherman became a hit.
The bald spot, fake hair, spray-on was his worst,
But still, he sold an awful lot of it.

The TV infomercial was his niche.
He starred as salesman and inventor, too.
"But wait. There's more." A phrase that made him rich,
Became his trademark as his stardom grew.

A legendary businessman indeed,
He made us purchase stuff we didn't need.

NEW YEAR'S EVE BALL DROP

An aging couple rarely stayed up late
But tried to last 'til midnight New Years Eve.
It simply got to be too long a wait,
A feat that they no longer could achieve.

In younger days, they might stay out 'til three.
They'd dine and dance. It wasn't hard at all.
But now they don't go out. They watch TV
And hope to see the dropping of the ball.

The ball drop signifies a brand-new year,
But most years they were sound asleep by ten.
Alas, as time went by, 'twas pretty clear
They'd never bring the new year in again.

So, they moved to Alaska. Now it's great.
They get to see the ball come down at eight.

CABLE TV NEWS

A guy stopped watching cable TV news.
Perspectives on the issues of the day
Depended on which network he would choose.
They'd differ greatly on what they would say.

Instead of getting mad, he's been amused.
Their aim is just to influence, it seems.
Small wonder channel flippers get confused.
Their minds get whipsawed by the two extremes.

He's old enough that he can still recall
When news was only on an hour a day.
The goal was to inform, and that was all.
Now blatant bias fills him with dismay.

The way the talking heads today behave,
Has Walter Cronkite turning in his grave.

BREAKING NEWS

A scary scene, police in riot gear.
A helicopter hovers overhead,
And down below, folks paralyzed with fear.
How many hurt? Is anybody dead?

A CNN crew hurries to the scene.
The local TV news teams got there first,
Reporting any info they could glean.
Their viewers couldn't help but fear the worst.

And caught up in the bedlam, there was you.
But you were calm. You'd seen it all before.
You understood exactly what to do.
'Twas brouhaha that you could just ignore.

A few arrests, and that would end it all.
A typical Black Friday at the mall.

Chapter 7

DEAR DIARY

Dear Diary
Chapter Notes

I have never kept a diary. If I had, I'm pretty certain the entries would not have been written in rhyming iambic pentameter. This chapter imagines what some of my entries might look like if I had actually kept a diary in that format. What's not imaginary are the stories themselves. These are all diary-worthy tales of actual thoughts or experiences, perhaps including a bit of exaggeration.

KNEW-IT-ALL

The smartest guy I ever knew was me,
But that was back when I was in my teens.
I wondered why my teachers couldn't see
That I'd been blessed with special genius genes.

The problems in the world did not seem large,
Though much too tough for leaders of the day.
I thought if they would just put me in charge,
I'd quickly make those troubles go away.

But all that brilliance faded through the years
Despite great lessons learned along the way.
I'm still an expert after several beers,
But mostly I've grown dumber day by day.

It's only when you've really learned a lot,
You start to realize how smart you're NOT !

CHEAP MOTEL

The lying neon sign read, "Clean and Cheap."
The pierced and tattooed desk clerk was a clue
This might not be a place I'd want to sleep,
But I was tired and any bed would do.

Or so I thought 'til I stepped through my door
To filthiness and stench that made me gag,
To giant roaches running 'cross the floor,
And to a concave bed with four inch sag.

But something good came from that awful night,
In spite of mouse turds on the bathroom floor,
Despite the burned-out bedside reading light.
'Twas then and there I vowed to sin no more.

I found religion in that cheap motel
For I had seen what housing's like in Hell.

SIRI

Since I met Siri, life has been so grand.
She gives directions, so I'm never lost.
There's dining information on demand,
And best of all, there's never any cost.

Each time I call she answers right away.
She's never moody, always super quick.
She's there for me all hours of the day.
I only have to talk, not type or click.

Though Apple tries to add things she can do,
She still can't reunite my orphan socks,
Or find lost keys and doesn't have a clue
If I ask her to pick some winning stocks.

We'll know that Siri's perfect version's here
When I can sit and have her fetch a beer.

SELF-DRIVING CARS

Should I acquire my own self-driving car?
Just how they work, I haven't got a clue.
I do think it would seem a bit bizarre
To sit there with no driving tasks to do.

Perhaps I'd read a book or take a snooze,
Or maybe I'd relax and have a beer,
Or watch TV, or catch up on the news.
I might enjoy the stress-free atmosphere.

But will it speed if I am late for work?
If cars ahead are pokey, will it pass?
And can it give the finger to a jerk?
Find parking spots? And fill itself with gas?

The scariest uncertainty by far:
Is it a frequently self-crashing car?

UNLUCKY IN LINE

Don't get behind me in a check-out line,
'Cuz I'm the guy who always has bad luck.
The other lines move twice as fast as mine.
Things happen up ahead to get me stuck.

I'll get behind some pokey coupon queen,
Or there's a standstill while they check a price,
Or have to change the tape in their machine,
Or call a supervisor for advice.

It's even worse at Starbuck's or the bank.
I absolutely hate the DMV.
While you might never wait to fill your tank,
There's always other cars ahead of me.

I dream about how life will be so fine,
When I can just do everything online.

THE UPS AND DOWNS OF CHURCH

Why is it we must stand so much in church?
We stand to sing, then sit, then stand some more.
The pastor from an elevated perch
Directs these movements we dare not ignore.

We rise to pray and hear the gospel read,
And then it's time to take a seat again.
Content to sit, we're asked to kneel instead.
Why can't we just get comfy now and then?

But what if church was like a football game?
Big plays alone make fans arise en masse.
Compared to touchdowns, church is pretty tame,
So don't expect that change will come to pass.

There's rationale involved, make no mistake.
It's by design to keep us all awake.

INSOMNIA

I lay awake one night and couldn't sleep.
My bedside clock read twenty after two.
I tried deep breathing, even counted sheep,
But neither worked. I wondered what to do.

At 5 AM I still was wide awake.
I fretted that without a good night's rest,
I'd doze at work. My job might be at stake!
So, I just lay there growing more depressed.

But my insomnia produced no harm.
The incident proved wondrously sublime.
I woke up to the sound of my alarm,
Well-rested at my ordinary time.

It shows events aren't always what they seem.
My sleeplessness was just a crazy dream.

ROBOTIC SLAVE

If I could have my own robotic slave,
He'd be a a guy. I think I'd name him Bob.
I'd have him cook whatever foods I'd crave
And take on every type of cleaning job.

A handy guy, he'd deal with all repairs,
Run Errands, cut the grass, and wash my cars.
He'd handle household bookkeeping affairs
And drive me home from parties and the bars.

But should I fear robotic servitude?
The key would be to have a good design
To program in an always docile mood
And intellect that's not as great as mine.

The awful situation I would dread:
He'd be so smart I'd work for him instead.

Chapter 8
ANIMALS WHO DRINK

Animals Who Drink
Chapter Notes

I am a fan of Gary Larson, the cartoonist who created "The Far Side." He often used talking animals, like dogs, cows, and other creatures as proxies for people to depict comical human behavior. The stories in this chapter use a variety of creatures to do much the same. The common thread is that they all behave like humans who have been drinking.

PIGS IN A BAR

Two half-drunk, full-grown pigs were in a bar
Discussing what the future held in store.
One said, "We shouldn't plan ahead too far.
Enjoy this day. We won't have many more."

He ordered several shots and raised some toasts.
He toasted first their imminent good-bye,
Then toasted bacon, pork chops, ham, and roasts.
The other pig said, "We don't have to die.

"I've come up with a plan I think you'll like.
They'll spare us if we lose a lot of weight.
We simply need to stage a hunger strike."
They did. It worked. It seemed they'd dodged their fate.

Alas, the gods of fate are sometimes mean.
When slaughtered they were sold as "Extra Lean".

CENTIPEDE KARAOKE

Two centipedes were drinking in a bar
And saw that it was karaoke night.
One told the other, "You could be the star."
The other said, "You're absolutely right.

"But first I need to drink a few more beers.
They're sure to make my courage level rise.
Just wait! You're gonna hear a bunch of cheers.
My dance moves guarantee I'll win the prize."

The show's emcee gave energetic praise,
And as a way to wish contestants luck,
He'd holler, "Break a leg!" the show biz phrase.
The centipede said, "All those others suck.

"And if I break a leg, I won't much care.
I've got another ninety-nine to spare."

ENDANGERED SPECIES

A prairie chicken and a long-eared bat
Were in a bar when they first got the word.
Their status as endangered, just like that,
Was gone…bad news they wished they hadn't heard.

"That's horrible," the shell-shocked chicken said,
"A crisis we'd be foolish to ignore.
I fear we both will likely end up dead.
Cuz we have human enemies galore."

"I fear you're right." replied the long-eared bat.
"Protections we've enjoyed no more apply.
They'll shoot you and destroy my habitat.
But we, at least, can choose the way we die.

So, I propose until our final breath
We sit right here and drink ourselves to death."

LIFE'S PURPOSE

Two gnats were drunk and talking in a bar.
Life's purpose was the topic of the day.
One said, "Life sucks. No matter where we are,
We're hated. People wish we'd go away.

"It seems we have no purpose on this earth.
Most creatures offer something they can give,
But we have zilch. Our species has no worth,
And if we did, three weeks is all we live."

"You sell us short." the other gnat replied.
"We're food for fish and birds. That's one good deed,
And we can claim another source of pride.
We satisfy a basic human need.

"Cuz humans love to grumble, groan, and pout.
Without us there'd be less to bitch about."

BAR FOOD

A termite and a mouse were in a bar
Consuming lots of beer and swapping yarns
About the places each has lived so far,
Including houses, churches, sheds, and barns.

The mouse said, "I enjoy a cozy house.
They're warm, and there are lots of things to eat."
"A barn," the termite said, "won't please a mouse,
But I like wood, so barns are hard to beat."

The barmaid overheard their talk of food
And said, "Our bar food choices are divine."
The mouse said, "I am really in the mood
For cheese curds," but his friend said "I'll decline.

"While items on your menu all look good,
This bar is made of oak. I'll just have wood."

MOSQUITO SCHOOL

Just graduated from a training school,
He'd learned survival tactics for a pest.
They taught that humans would be very cruel
And safe-to-bite locations that are best.

They warned him of the places NOT to bite.
Stay off the arms, and don't go near the head.
The back is best because it's out of sight
And hard for them to reach to slap you dead.

The grads all partied hard. He drank a lot,
Then went to find a human to attack.
Alas, in his condition he forgot
And bit him on the forearm, not the back.

And so, despite the knowledge he'd amassed,
His first bite also proved to be his last.

THE TORTOISE AND THE HARE

A tortoise and a hare were in a bar.
Half-plastered, they discussed their fabled race.
The hare, although much speedier by far,
Was beaten by a slow but steady pace.

"I want a rematch," said the angry hare.
"You drugged my carrots so I'd fall asleep.
If we can have a race that's fair and square,
I'll kick your butt, you pokey, cheatin' creep."

The tortoise said, "No rules were specified
So you've no right my tactics to assail."
"Your win," the hare said, "should be nullified,
Or else let's change the moral of this tale.

"Let's switch from 'Slow and steady wins the race'
To 'Those who cheat to win are a disgrace.'"

COCKROACH ENVY

Two cockroaches were drinking in a bar.
They'd heard the news about their former friend.
Success in life had taken him quite far.
Alas, a boot stomp brought it to an end.

The first roach said, "That would have been a shame
Except he changed and turned into a jerk.
'Twas luck alone that brought him wealth and fame.
He never did a day of honest work."

"I wish I had his luck." the other said.
"His ego got too big. I'll shed no tears.
He dumped his friends. Success went to his head.
Let's celebrate." He ordered two more beers.

'Tis much like humans act. Perhaps we all
Rejoice when folks we envy take a fall.

SKUNKS IN A BAR

Two skunks, the night before Thanksgiving Day,
Were sitting on two barstools in a bar.
One said, "I hate how others move away
To flee from us, no matter where we are."

His friend, who hadn't had as much to drink,
Said, "Just be thankful. Skunks should all be proud.
We're chosen ones by God who get to stink.
Rejoice, we're never crowded in a crowd.

"And best of all, our sense of smell is bad,
So we are not aware of our own scent .
And our smell's not the worst. You should be glad."
Just then a man walked in, a smelly gent.

He'd passed some really noxious gas that proved
Skunks aren't the worst. They both got up and moved.

Chapter 9

PHOBIAS

Phobias
Chapter Notes

A sore shoulder that led to rotator cuff surgery for me was preceded by an MRI. Getting into that little tube was not enjoyable and made me realize I am claustrophobic. But it inspired me to spend some of my surgery recovery time writing sonnets about other types of phobias. Brace yourself for some dark humor, laced with irony.

AEROPHOBIA...FEAR OF FLYING

A lady who was terrified to fly
Would only go to places in her car.
She feared the plane would crash and she would die,
Which meant she never traveled very far.

She yearned for places she would never go
Unless she somehow overcame her fear.
But then a hypnotist she came to know
Said, "I can make that problem disappear."

For weeks, they worked together every day.
He taught her how to self-induce a trance.
It made her trepidation go away
And made her brave enough to take a chance.

So, off she flew, assured by what she'd learned.
An hour in, the airplane crashed and burned.

PLASMOPHOBIA......FEAR OF GHOSTS

He thought he saw a ghost when he was eight,
And ghosts have scared him ever since that day,
A phobia his wife had grown to hate.
She vowed to help him make it go away.

To change his mind about the ghosts he feared,
She took him to a graveyard late at night,
Then to a seance, but no ghosts appeared.
Confronting fear had rid him of his fright.

She bragged to friends how she'd achieved success.
Alas, next night when she had gone to bed,
She woke to terror she could not suppress,
A visit from a person long since dead.

The tables turned, she now regrets those boasts,
For she's the one who now is scared of ghosts.

COULROPHOBIA......FEAR OF CLOWNS

A little girl once had a scary dream.
A clown had used an axe to kill her cat.
It caused her to awaken with a scream,
And she was clownophobic after that.

'Twas just a dream, but ever since that night,
She lived in fear, and though 'twas asinine,
The thought of clowns brought paralyzing fright.
The ghastliness sent shivers up her spine.

Her parents hired a shrink to calm her fears.
It worked. Her fear of clowns had gone away.
She hadn't thought about a clown in years
Until one showed up at her door one day.

She should have hid but let him in instead.
He hit her with his axe, and now she's dead.

OPHIDIOPHOBIA......FEAR OF SNAKES

A lady had a deathly fear of snakes.
'Twas real and caused anxiety so great,
The very thought of them gave her the shakes
And always made her hyperventilate.

She joined a group of folks who shared her fear.
They claimed to have an innovative coach.
Her first encounter made it very clear
He took a very radical approach.

They met inside a snake infested pit,
Watched deadly vipers slither 'cross the floor
And heard from other members who'd been bit.
In just two minutes she was out the door.

While thoughts of snakes still leave her feeling stressed,
Support group fears cause even more unrest.

HYDROPHOBIA.....FEAR OF WATER

He watched a famous movie and got scared.
A wet witch melted in the final scene.
"I'll never go in water," he declared.
His fear had changed his family's routine.

He wouldn't bathe, was terrified to swim,
And even turned down water for his thirst.
His mother wondered, "What's come over him?"
And vowed to get his phobia reversed.

Her coaxing failed to lessen his distress.
She took him to famous, high-priced shrink.
It took some time, but he achieved success,
And when the boy got brave enough to drink,

He stared melting, then dissolved some more
And ended up a puddle on the floor.

NOMOPHOBIA VICTIM

He's like a stalker watching night and day.
Folks comment how they've seen him stare at me.
It's like I'm trapped and just can't get away.
I wish he'd take a break and let me be.

I hate it when it's time to go to bed.
I know he's watching. It's so hard to sleep.
I wish he'd go lurk somewhere else instead.
He runs my life. The guy's a total creep.

Perhaps it's mental illness, some disease.
He might be harmless. I don't really care.
I only know I'm always ill at ease.
I'm going crazy from his constant stare.

I wish the jerk would just leave me alone.
He's phone addicted. Sadly, I'm his phone.

Note: Nomophobia is the modern fear of being detached
from mobile phone connectivity.

.

Chapter 10
QUIRKY PEOPLE

Quirky People
Chapter Notes

The dictionary definition of quirky is "strikingly unconventional." It would be hard to describe any of the folks you'll meet in this chapter as conventional. Some are amusing, others annoying. A few might even remind you of people you know.

ACRONYM ADDICT

The language shortcut that initials take
Was something that had great appeal to him.
He'd formed a habit that he couldn't break.
He loved to make a phrase an acronym.

This started causing problems in his life.
It led to being ostracized at work.
It strained relations with his kids and wife.
He seemed possessed. Friends thought he'd gone berserk.

A newly forming group had caught his eye.
He'd get support from addicts like himself.
But their first meeting sadly went awry,
And all their lofty plans went on the shelf.

The group dissolved. They'd failed in their aim
To give the group an acronymic name.

CRAZY CHICKEN LADY

It wasn't like a normal poultry farm.
Her chickens were not raised for folks to eat.
She pampered them and sheltered them from harm.
She gave them back rubs and massaged their feet.

'Twas all a plan designed their trust to earn,
So she might come at last to know the truth.
She hoped from them the answers she might learn
To questions that had plagued her since her youth.

To find out why the chicken crossed the road
And which came first? The chicken or the egg?
Alas, the birds seemed stuck in silent mode
And gave no clues, despite how much she'd beg.

So, answers still are shrouded in mystique,
For chickens have no lips and cannot speak.

SPORTS FANATIC

A sports bar was his frequent viewing place.
He'd wear the jersey of his cherished team.
He'd also paint their colors on his face,
And pound the bar, drink beer, and yell, and scream.

He'd sometimes buy the cheapest nose-bleed seat
To watch firsthand and help them with his cheers.
The mancave in his home could not be beat
For watching games while drinking cheaper beers.

He never missed a game, and when they won,
"Euphoric" was the best word for his mood.
But when they lost, his wife and dog would run.
They feared his rage. He always came unglued.

Too often peoples' moods go to extremes
Because of wins or losses by their teams.

COMPULSIVE CONFORMIST

A lady cared about what others thought,
But agonized about it to extreme.
Approval of her acts was what she sought.
Without it she could have no self-esteem.

Convinced all eyes were watching every move,
She lived her life expressly to conform.
Her constant fear was folks would disapprove
Of any deviation from the norm.

She didn't know she didn't need to bear
The worry, fear, and torturous self-doubt
'Cuz other people rarely really care.
Their own concerns are what they fret about.

What others think should never make us fuss.
They hardly ever even think of us.

INTELLIGENCE NOT REQUIRED

He's not the brightest bulb in the marquis
And not the sharpest crayon in the box.
A crumpet short of hosting folks for tea,
He's barely smarter than a box of rocks.

His brain fits in his head with room to spare.
The rest is like a belfry full of bats.
A chopstick short of eating with a pair,
His thoughts are scattered, like a herd of cats.

But even though he's dumber than a stump,
He still enjoys a happy, thriving life,
A life that's undeserved for such a chump,
Nice home, good job, cute kids, and gorgeous wife.

Success came not from anything he's done.
He's just a wealthy, business owner's son.

REVERSAL OF FORTUNE

His life was like a melancholic song,
A loser ever since he was a kid.
No matter what he tried, it turned out wrong.
Success evaded everything he did.

Devoid of skills, good looks, and intellect,
He couldn't hold a job or make a friend.
Why people treated him with disrespect
Is not a baffling thing to comprehend.

But then one day he played the Power Ball.
That night he checked what numbers had been drawn.
In shock, he saw his ticket matched them all.
It looked as if those loser days were gone.

Alas, in truth, 'twas not his lucky day.
Within a year, he'd pissed it all away.

POSSUM COUNTY BEAUTY PAGEANT

Earlene thought she should be Miss Tennessee
But had to win a local contest first.
The Possum County Pageant was to be
Her start or where she'd get her bubble burst.

She should have said she'd work for world peace
But pledged instead to get the sheriff fired.
And though she'd always been a bit obese,
She wore a swimsuit smaller than required.

Her lip-synch talent act was truly bad
While one gal had a lovely singing voice.
You couldn't blame the crowd for being mad
To hear Earlene proclaimed the judge's choice.

The runner-up will always hold a grudge.
Turns out Earlene was sleeping with the judge.

ONE-UPPER

You couldn't tell a tale he couldn't top.
One-upping was his most annoying trait.
To show you up he'd blabber on nonstop.
If you did something good, he did it great.

You caught a three-pound fish, but his weighed four.
Your trip was cool, but his made yours look lame.
Your taxes are too high, but his are more.
Your dog is smart, but his puts yours to shame.

In truth, he's been inclined to twist the facts.
He's really just an ordinary guy
Who magnifies his ordinary acts.
He's friendless, but he's clueless as to why.

It's very clear that he's oblivious
To something that should be quite obvious.

WEIRD NAMES FOR KIDS

The parents of a newborn baby boy
Decided that his name should be unique.
Since breakfast is a meal they both enjoy,
They named him Oatmeal, thinking it was chic.

As other kids were born, they kept that theme.
A daughter, Omelette, was their second born.
Twins, Toast and Pancake, fit the naming scheme,
But all were doomed to ridicule and scorn.

In school, the kids were taunted, teased and mocked.
The names their folks had once considered cool
Caused incidents that left the parents shocked.
They'd not foreseen how kids can be so cruel.

When christened with a quirky, offbeat name,
If kids get bullied, parents are to blame.

BEAR COSTUME

A man who had a quirky sense of fun
Would frequently impersonate a bear.
His costume was a cheap and tacky one.
It made folks laugh and wasn't meant to scare.

But then he bought a realistic suit
Which proved to be a terrible mistake.
His bear resemblance was so absolute
That no one knew the costume was a fake.

A frightened neighbor called the DNR
Who shot him with a tranquilizer dart.
They took him to the zoo to be a star,
And foolishly he tried to play the part.

Until a real bear thinking this was great
Decided, sadly, he was there to mate.

COLD FEET

A redneck bride was walking down the aisle.
The wedding party saw her face turn red.
A look of great alarm replaced her smile,
As out the door the redneck bridegroom fled.

A short time later, she received this text:
"I never thought that I would get cold feet.
We need to figure out what happens next.
I'm down at Bubba's Bar. How 'bout we meet?"

She'd felt humiliation when he left,
Her need to get revenge was very strong,
The antidote for feeling so bereft
Was poison in his beer to right the wrong.

With even colder feet, her former beau
Lies in the morgue, a name tag on his toe.

END OF THE WORLD GUY

He walked around and held a sign that read,
"The end of life on Earth will come this week."
But when all Earthlings failed to end up dead,
Folks labeled him a weirdo, crackpot freak.

Yet, every week the sign and he were back.
For twenty years, his message was the same.
Ignored by most, a few would give him flack,
But over time, he gained a bit of fame.

Oft challenged by the folks from TV news,
He'd say, "Each week a million people die.
To prove my point, that fact's the one I choose.
I'm right each week, and here's the reason why:

That everyone would die, I've never said,
I'm talking 'bout the million newly dead."

Chapter 11
From the Stump

From The Stump
Chapter Notes

It will become obvious in the following stories that I like to pick on politicians, and they are a pretty easy target. Rather than be outraged by the behavior of these folks, my blood pressure is reduced by looking for humor in what can be pretty upsetting. I'm not a fan of either Trump or Biden and have tried to poke fun at them in equal measure. There are also couple of rants about distracted drivers and graffiti, neither of which I find amusing.

CONGRESSIONAL TERM LIMITS

Elected politicians serve too long,
A lot like pigs who linger at the trough.
We ought to change our laws to right this wrong
And spell out rules for when they must step off.

Let's cap the Senate's six-year terms at two.
The two-year House terms ought to change to four,
But three terms should be all that they can do,
Though many current members might serve more.

Exempting current members from the bill
Would be the way that change could come to pass.
In time, we'd get the lifers off the hill
And clean up this inhibiting morass.

We need to make the pattern disappear
Of having people make it a career.

ELECTION CAMPAIGN ADS

Don't vote for my opponent. He's a Jerk.
He cheats on both his taxes and his wife.
He's never done a day of honest work.
He ought to be in prison doing life!

He flips and flops on issues that are hot.
His mind seems like it's always in a fog.
No doubt that's 'cuz he smokes a lot of pot.
Surveillance photos show he kicks his dog.

Are we not sick of ads that sound like this?
Elections have become a slimy game.
We're falling deeper into this abyss.
Politicos and voters both share blame.

As long as sleaze is how the votes are won,
A lot of folks we should elect won't run.

CONGRESSIONAL OATH OF OFFICE

With hand on heart, I make this solemn vow
To treat the other party with disdain
And stretch beyond the bounds the rules allow
To help the folks who give to my campaign.

For any goal I'm driven to achieve,
I pledge to hoodwink, dupe, betray, and lie.
I'll master skills required to deceive.
Misconduct allegations I'll deny.

And when opponents try to win my seat,
I'll use all means to fend off their attacks.
I swear that I won't hesitate to cheat
By hiding awkward truths and twisting facts.

Recurring re-election is my goal,
And so, I hereby pledge to sell my soul.

TRUMP PLAYS GOLF

He took a gimme on a ten-foot putt
And kicked his ball from out behind a tree.
In truth, he scored at least a seven, but
His scorecard says he somehow made a three.

He hit a ball that landed in the sand.
Since sand shots are a weakness in his game,
To get it out, he tossed it with his hand.
For folks who play like this there is a name.

They're Golf Cheats, undeserving of respect
And doomed to spend eternity in hell.
They can't be trusted, and as you'd expect,
They'll cheat at many other things as well.

In business, politics, and on his wife,
For Donald, cheating's been a way of life.

SLEEPY JOE

He's got by far the toughest job on earth,
Impossible for even younger folks.
As people now evaluate his worth,
Seems Sleepy Joe's become the butt of jokes.

He stammers when he talks. He trips on stairs.
He seems worn out and nearly obsolete.
He falls asleep in comfy meeting chairs.
There's pee on every White House toilet seat.

A cane, a walker, then a wheelchair?
Glaucoma, hearing loss, a balding dome?
A growing staff of doctors giving care?
The White House might become a nursing home.

A scary world in which the stakes are high,
It's way too much for any feeble guy.

A BIT LIKE SCROOGE

As Donald Trump lay sleeping in his bed,
The Ghost of Business Past paid him a call.
He said, "You've used deceit to get ahead.
You're wealthy, but I've come to seize it all."

Appearing next, the Ghost of Lechery
Reviewed his many episodes of lust.
She told him, "For your carnal treachery,
I'll castrate you, a punishment that's just."

By morning, he'd encountered three more ghosts,
The Ghost of Lying, Ghost of Shifting Blame,
And Ghost of Irritating Twitter Posts.
Each chastised him as one by one they came.

When Donald woke, he found 'twas just a dream,
But still he fired his Secret Service Team.

TOO OLD TO RUN

As POTUS Joe lay sleeping in his bed,
The Ghost of Past Elections paid a call.
At first, he thought that Sleepy Joe was dead.
He wasn't showing signs of life at all.

When woken, he was asked, "Are you OK?"
A groggy Joe replied, "What brings you here?"
The ghost said, "I've advice for you today.
Don't run again. It won't go well, I fear.

"The voters think you're old and out of touch.
You're feeble, shaky, faltering, and frail.
Your former backers now don't like you much.
If you don't step aside, you're doomed to fail.

"By twenty twenty-eight, you might be dead.
You really ought to quit while you're ahead."

DISTRACTED DRIVERS

Cops seldom bust them, but they're everywhere,
Distracted drivers on our roads and streets.
They put on makeup, floss, and comb their hair
While posting Instagrams and Twitter tweets.

They check their email, blabber on their phones,
Drink coffee, eat, watch videos, and read.
They zoom through school and road construction zones.
They weave and can't maintain a steady speed.

Although 'tis much in vogue to multi-task,
There's danger in temptations that distract.
Is wanting safer roads too much to ask?
This problematic threat should be attacked.

The penalty, if I had any say,
Would be to take their phones and cars away.

GRAFFITI....IS IT ART?

Graffiti seems to show up everywhere.
A building, fence, a railroad car, or wall
Becomes a canvas when there's spray paint there.
It sometimes shows up in a bathroom stall.

The images are like some secret code.
Their alphabet's a mystery to me.
The painters work in late-night, outlaw mode,
And when they see a cop, they have to flee.

Some call it art; most others disagree.
Creators sometimes demonstrate great skill.
True artists though, don't choose to work for free
Or stick somebody with clean-up bill.

As fine art knowledge goes, I'm not real smart,
But I know vandalism isn't art.

THEY'RE FOUND IN EVERY CROWD

At movies, concerts, ball games. and at plays,
We're apt to find those people who annoy.
They never fail to find a host of ways
The happiness of others to destroy.

Except for times we're s'posed to laugh or clap,
A theatre should be a quiet zone.
Yet, there's the gal who just can't shut her yap
Or some guy who forgets to mute his phone.

Exuberance at concerts or a game
Is normal, But the folks who block your view
By never sitting ought to feel some shame,
As should the guy who spills a beer on you.

A special seating section for the jerks
Perhaps might be a remedy that works.

Chapter 12
Misfits

Misfits
Chapter Notes

When putting this book together, I started by making hard copies of all the sonnets and putting them into piles related to various themes. Each pile became a chapter. Then, Joella Goyette created illustrations to introduce the themes of those chapters. But there were some leftover sonnets that didn't fit neatly with any particular theme. So, the only common denominator of the stories in this final chapter is that they are all misfits.

MIDLIFE CRISIS....THE MUSICAL

A midlife crisis show has made the news,
Attracting huge, adoring, Broadway throngs.
A musical, it's getting rave reviews,
And here's its list of clever, catchy songs.

"I Dyed My Hair." "I Love My New Corvette."
"She Likes to Flirt." "We Both Stayed Late at Work."
"She's Half My Age." "A Night I Won't Forget."
"My Wife Found Out." "My Kids Think I'm A Jerk."

"She Broke It Off." "Oh, no! What Have I done?"
"Her Lawyer Called." "My Stuff Is in The Street."
"Regrets And Shame." "It Wasn't Worth the Fun."
"I Wish She'd Take Me Back." "Twas Wrong to Cheat."

"I'm Screwed." "Some Bad Decisions Made in Haste."
"I've Learned My Brain Is Not Below My Waist"

COFFEE SNOBS

For some folks, Folgers brewed at home will do,
And others drink employers' workplace stuff.
With scorn, such options coffee snobs pooh-pooh.
Barista drinks alone are good enough.

A Starbucks fix is never far away.
Each morning coffee snobs will stand in line.
Without caffein as fuel to start the day,
These groggy folks might rise but wouldn't shine.

The dollars spent each day accumulate
To totals coffee snobs don't care to know.
The cost in terms of time might be as great,
Especially on those days the line is slow.

These folks create a lot of millionaires,
Investors who own lots of Starbucks shares.

GENIE IN A BOTTLE

A grateful genie who a guy had freed
Said, "Make a wish. I'll see that it comes true."
The guy said, " Great! I'll tell you what I need.
I think a hundred wishes ought to do."

The guy began to list what he desired:
A million bucks, a house, a brand-new car.
He added. "I would like to be retired.
No wait, I want to be a movie star."

The guy went on. The genie yelled, "Enough!
Why must you genie helpers be such fools?
Wish all you want, but you won't get that stuff.
To wish for extra wishes breaks the rules.

"I'll hear no more. Your wishing time is done.
The choice you made rescinds your only one."

INSULT ARTIST

A politician slammed his longtime foe.
"The guy's the south end of a northbound horse.
He's bribable. His vote's for sale, you know.
The highest bidder always wins, of course.

The male offspring of a female dog,
He's never done a day of honest work"
Were things he'd said about him on his blog.
He added, "He's a moron and a jerk."

When criticized for badmouthing the guy,
He said, "It's not disparagement if true.
I'm not afraid to look him in the eye
And tell him he's a drunken scumbag. too.

In calling him these names, I've no remorse
Except they're insults to the dog and horse".

REJUVANEX

Rejuvanex, your path to better days,
A miracle on which you can depend.
Its benefits have earned it lavish praise,
A regimen that doctors recommend.

Rejuvanex defends against disease,
Builds stronger bones, reduces A1C,
Controls cholesterol, and guarantees
You won't believe the weight loss you will see.

And though it offers benefits galore,
Prescriptions for it never are required.
And don't expect to find it in a store.
It's not a drug or thing to be acquired.

If you're astute, perhaps you will surmise
It's just a made-up name for exercise.

Biography

Ken Mogren has been a nearly lifelong resident of Winona, MN, in the beautiful Mississippi River Valley. At Winona State University, he majored in Psychology and English and credits an understanding of human nature and good communication skills for success in a 43-year insurance industry career.

At about age 60, he rekindled a dormant interest in creative writing and began entering humorous sonnets in contests, enjoying a bit of success. In retirement he has picked up the pace, resulting in a collection of over 200 sonnets.

Ken and his wife, Sally, enjoy traveling and spending time with their three sons and their families. He also serves as a volunteer on the non-profit boards of a hospital, university and theatre company. Ken's other interests include running, cycling, and cross-country skiing. He regularly competes in those sports and has won three national age group championships. He also enjoys kayaking and golf.

Printed in the USA
CPSIA information can be obtained
at www.ICGtesting.com
CBHW051627060724
11222CB00035B/1066